Angela Royston

Wild Weather
HURRICANES and TORNADOES

QED Publishing

ISBN 978 1 84538 968 0

Printed and bound in China

Author Angela Royston
Consultant Terry Jennings
Editor Amanda Askew
Designer Mo Choy
Picture Researcher Claudia Tate
Illustrator Julian Baker

Publisher Steve Evans
Creative Director Zeta Davies

Picture credits (a=above, b=below)
Alamy A T Willett 5a, A T Willett 19a, A T Willett 19b, Mary Evans Picture Library 25b

Corbis Daniel Aguilar/Reuters 5b, Jim Reed 9b, Bettmann 11a, 11b NOAA/Handout/
Reuters, Mike Theiss/Ultimate Chase 12, Paul Buck/epa 13l, Smiley N Pool/Dallas
Morning News 13r, Steven Clevenger 14, Reuters 15l, Tom Bean 16, Jim Reed 20,
Jim Reed 21b, R H Productions/Robert Harding World Imagery 24, Car Culture 29a

Getty Images Paul & Lindamarie Ambrose 1, 9a, AFP 15r, Jim Reed 18, AFP 22, 23b,
Tui De Roy 25a, AFP 26, 27a, 27b

Science Photolibrary Larry Miller 21a

Shutterstock Franc Podgor 4, Mushin 7, Zastol`skiy Victor Leonidovich 10a,
Jhaz Photography 17, Michael Klenetsky 23a, Rafal Olkis 29b

Words in **bold** can be found in the glossary on page 30.

Contents

Hurricanes and tornadoes

Hurricanes and tornadoes are dangerous weather that can kill people and animals, and damage farm **crops**, buildings and other property. Tornadoes whip up the strongest winds on Earth.

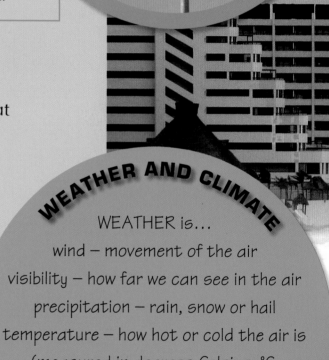

▶ An anemometer is an instrument that measures the speed of the wind.

HURRICANES

A hurricane is a huge storm with violent winds that develops over the ocean. Winds of more than 120 kilometres an hour and heavy rain clouds swirl around the centre of the hurricane, which is called the 'eye'. The eye is an area of stillness and calm. The storm, which can be hundreds of kilometres wide, moves across the ocean. A hurricane becomes stronger as it travels over warmer water towards the coast. When a hurricane hits land, it quickly loses its strength because the ocean provides it with the energy and moisture it needs to exist. A hurricane wreaks damage across a wide area, causing the most destruction on islands and in coastal areas.

WEATHER AND CLIMATE

WEATHER is...
wind – movement of the air
visibility – how far we can see in the air
precipitation – rain, snow or hail
temperature – how hot or cold the air is
(measured in degrees Celsius, °C,
or degrees Fahrenheit, °F)
CLIMATE is the average weather
a place gets over a long
period of time.

TORNADOES

A tornado is a storm with violently rotating wind. It looks like **funnel**-shaped cloud. A tornado usually develops under a big **thundercloud**. It does not last long but its winds are often much faster and stronger than those of a hurricane – they can reach 500 kilometres an hour. The biggest tornadoes are 1.5 kilometres wide, but most are less than 500 metres wide. A tornado can destroy everything in its narrow path.

▲ A tornado forms as a thin funnel under a heavy thundercloud.

▼ Hurricane Andrew hit Miami in Florida, USA, on 23 August 1992.

What is wind?

Wind is air moving across the surface of the Earth, as a gentle breeze or a strong wind. Wind is caused by the Sun heating some parts of the Earth more than others. As the ground warms up, it heats the air above. The warm air then rises and cooler air rushes in. The faster the warm air rises, the faster cooler air moves in and so the stronger the wind.

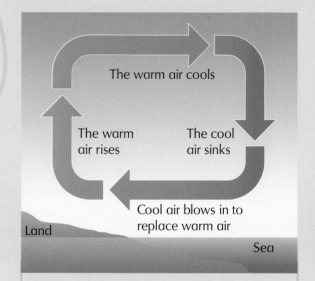

The warm air cools

The warm air rises

The cool air sinks

Cool air blows in to replace warm air

Land

Sea

▲ Warm air rises, pulling in cooler air to take its place. The rising air cools and falls back towards the Earth's surface.

RECORD WIND

The highest wind speed ever recorded is 372 kilometres an hour, on Mount Washington, USA, in 1934. The worst tornadoes may produce winds of 500 kilometres an hour, but their speeds have never been accurately measured.

▼ The main prevailing winds blow towards the Equator, and towards the North and South poles.

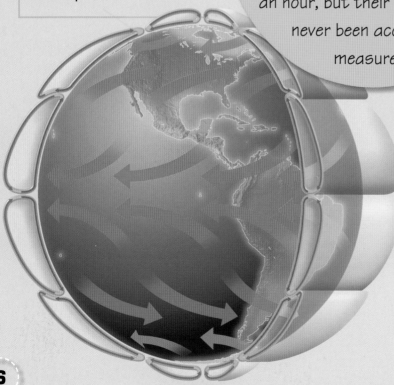

PREVAILING WINDS

In most places, the wind blows from one direction most of the time. This is called a **prevailing wind** and it varies in different parts of the world. For example, in the tropics, prevailing winds blow towards the **Equator.** The Sun's rays are strongest over the Equator and so as hot air rises, cooler air from the north and south is pulled in. The cooler air forms the prevailing winds.

BEAUFORT SCALE

STRENGTH	WIND SPEED	EFFECT
0 Calm	0 kilometres an hour	Chimney smoke rises straight up
1 Light air	1–5 kilometres an hour	Smoke drifts gently
2 Light breeze	6–11 kilometres an hour	Leaves rustle, wind felt on face
3 Gentle breeze	12–19 kilometres an hour	Leaves and twigs on trees move
4 Moderate breeze	20–29 kilometres an hour	Small branches move
5 Fresh breeze	30–39 kilometres an hour	Small trees start to sway
6 Strong breeze	40–50 kilometres an hour	Large branches move
7 Near gale	51–61 kilometres an hour	Whole trees sway
8 Gale	62–74 kilometres an hour	Twigs broken off trees
9 Severe gale	75–87 kilometres an hour	Small branches and tiles blown off
10 Storm	88–102 kilometres an hour	Houses damaged, trees blown down
11 Severe storm	103–120 kilometres an hour	Serious damage
12 Hurricane	120 kilometres an hour +	Widespread damage

LOCAL WINDS

Winds are affected by the landscape. High mountainsides get more wind than low-lying land in **valleys**. Similarly, places along the coast or beside large lakes are often windy. Land warms up and cools down faster than water. During the day, when the land becomes much warmer than the sea, the wind blows from the sea to the land. The opposite happens at night – the land is cooler than the sea, so the wind blows from the land to the sea. The force of the wind is measured by the **Beaufort scale**.

▶ It is easy to see which way the prevailing wind blows on this hillside – the trees have grown away from the wind.

Where do severe storms occur?

Hurricanes and tornadoes can happen in most parts of the world, but they are most frequent in particular places at particular times of the year. Hurricanes usually start as **tropical** storms, which form over warm water near the Equator. They are pushed hundreds of kilometres across the sea by prevailing winds. Tornadoes form below severe thunderstorms.

▼ Severe storms are called hurricanes, **typhoons** and **cyclones** in different parts of the world.

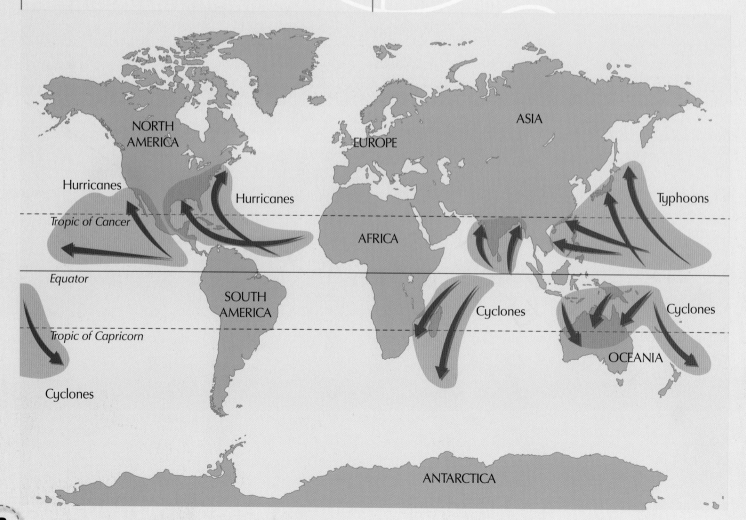

TROPICAL STORMS

Hurricane, typhoon and cyclone are different names for severe tropical storms. Hurricanes form over the Atlantic Ocean and move towards the Caribbean Sea and the Gulf of Mexico. They occur between May and October. Storms that form in the eastern Pacific Ocean, north of the Equator are also called hurricanes. Typhoons form in the northwest Pacific Ocean and are most frequent in summer. They strike countries from the Philippines to Japan. Cyclones form in the southern Pacific Ocean and Indian Ocean. They hit countries from Bangladesh, in the northern Indian Ocean, to Mozambique in east Africa, and Australia.

TORNADO ALLEY

Tornadoes can form almost anywhere, but the United States gets more tornadoes than anywhere else in the world – about 800 a year. Most of these are in 'Tornado Alley', an area in the Great Plains region that stretches from the state of Texas to South Dakota. Australia gets the second most tornadoes each year, but Bangladesh, China, India and England are hit frequently, too.

▶ Many houses in Qianzhang village in south-eastern China were destroyed by Typhoon Saomai in August 2006. It was the worst typhoon for 50 years.

TYPHOON

In the past, people explained storms and wild weather through myths and the gods. In Greece, Typhoon was a gigantic monster with 100 heads, who terrified the gods. He was killed by Zeus but his sons, the storm winds, survived.

▼ Meteorologists watch a large thunderstorm in Tornado Alley to see if a tornado will develop below it.

How does a hurricane form?

A hurricane begins over an ocean, about 50 to 100 kilometres north or south of the Equator. It forms when a tropical storm moves over an area of rising warm, moist air. The storm becomes stronger, causing winds to spiral faster around its centre.

SWIRLING WINDS

A hurricane forms above the ocean where the temperature of the sea is more than 27 degrees Celsius. Water evaporates and the warm, moist air quickly expands and rises. This pulls in strong winds of cooler air underneath. The spin of the Earth causes the winds to rotate. North of the Equator, the winds spin anti-clockwise and south of the Equator, they move clockwise. The winds spin around the centre, called the eye. The strongest winds are closest to the eye, in the **eyewall**.

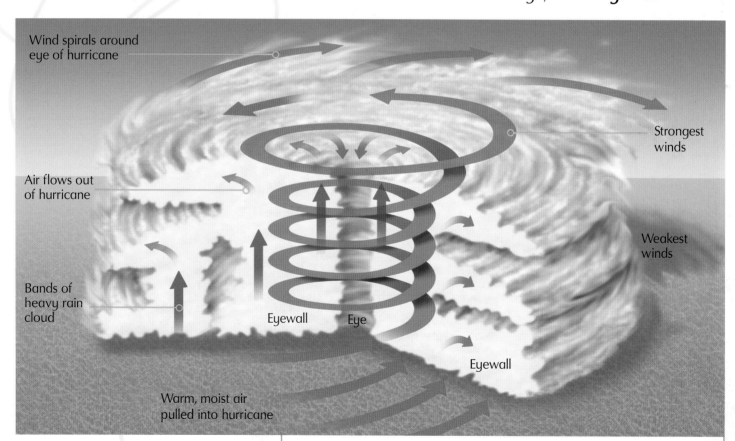

Wind spirals around eye of hurricane

Air flows out of hurricane

Bands of heavy rain cloud

Warm, moist air pulled into hurricane

Eyewall

Eye

Eyewall

Strongest winds

Weakest winds

▲ A hurricane consists of a huge spiral of strong winds and rain. The eye at the centre of the hurricane is an area of calm.

▲ A hurricane hunter flies into the eye of a hurricane to photograph the eyewall.

TRACKING A HURRICANE

Some hurricanes disappear before they reach land. Others become stronger as they move over warmer water. In the Atlantic Ocean and northern Pacific Ocean, the strength of a hurricane is rated according to the **Saffir-Simpson scale**. Scientists called meteorologists use weather balloons, **radar** and weather satellites to look for new hurricanes. Hurricane hunters are special aircraft that fly right into the eye of a hurricane to measure its strength. Photos taken by weather satellites help meteorologists to track its route.

▶ A photograph of Hurricane Katrina taken by a **weather satellite** on 29 August 2005, just as the hurricane hit New Orleans.

SAFFIR-SIMPSON SCALE

STRENGTH	WIND SPEED	DAMAGE
1 Weak	119–153 kilometres an hour	Some damage to signs and caravans
2 Moderate	154–177 kilometres an hour	Considerable damage to caravans, some damage to roofs and trees
3 Strong	178–209 kilometres an hour	Large trees blown over, caravans destroyed, damage to buildings, flooding
4 Very strong	210–249 kilometres an hour	Much damage to buildings, roofs blown off
5 Devastating	249 kilometres an hour +	Severe damage to buildings, small buildings blown away, coastal flooding

Preparing for a hurricane

A hurricane takes several days to develop and move across the ocean before it reaches land. This gives meteorologists time to warn people who live in its path. However, a hurricane can change its direction, or course, at any time, so it is difficult to predict exactly where it will strike the coast.

NAMING HURRICANES

Hurricanes are given names. The first hurricane of the season is given a name beginning with A, the second with B, and so on. The first six names for hurricanes in the Atlantic Ocean in 2010 are Alex, Bonnie, Colin, Danielle, Earl and Fiona.

▲ These people were still on the street when Hurricane Katrina hit Florida, USA. They are in serious danger of being blown away or hit by flying **debris**.

HURRICANE WARNING

Most countries have a system of hurricane warnings. In the United States, a hurricane warning means that a hurricane is likely in the next 24 hours. People listen to their radios and television for the most up-to-date news. They bring in patio furniture and other loose things that are outside. Offices, schools and other organizations stop work so people can go home.

STORM APPROACHING

As the storm gets nearer, people pull shutters down over their windows or cover them with wood to stop the glass being broken by the wind. If their homes are strongly built and unlikely to **flood**, some people may decide to stay there during the storm. If so, they have to keep away from windows and doors connecting to the outside. In many areas, however, people will be told to **evacuate**, or leave, their homes. They have to move to somewhere safer inland. Then they pack essential things and join the long queues of traffic leaving the coast.

▶ Traffic filled both sides of the highway when Galveston was evacuated before Hurricane Rita hit land on 24 September 2005.

▲ Covering windows with wood stops them being broken during a hurricane.

13

Destructive power

Hurricanes bring three forces of destruction – strong winds, heavy rain and high seas. As the storm approaches, the wind becomes stronger and the rains heavier. When the eye of the storm passes over, the wind and rain stop completely.

▲ Water flooded the streets of New Orleans after Hurricane Katrina hit the city on 29 August 2005.

WIND AND RAIN

Hurricanes are rated according to their strength. Trees, caravans and cars are easily damaged by wind. Shop signs, rubbish bins and anything that is not securely fixed may be tossed about by the wind. Trees bend and their branches break off. In the strongest hurricanes, whole trees are uprooted, roofs are blown off houses and, unless they are strongly built, whole houses are blown over. Heavy rain fills rivers and drains, which can overflow and cause flooding. The worst flooding in a hurricane is caused by the sea.

STORM SURGE

The rising air around the centre of a hurricane makes the sea below it bulge upwards. When it blows towards the land, the bulge can be more than 6 metres in height. This is called a **storm surge**. When the hurricane hits the coast, the storm surge raises the level of the sea. The strong winds whip up giant waves that crash onto the shore. Unless the coast has good **flood defences**, the waves flood the land. They can push boats far inland and wash cars and debris into the sea.

▼ Massive waves battered the coast of Cuba during Hurricane Rita in September 2005.

▲ In May 2008, Cyclone Nargis swept through Burma, killing thousands of people and destroying villages and towns. Here families on Haing Guy Island are trying to dry out what remains of their possessions.

Thunderstorms

Hurricanes often include thunderstorms, and most tornadoes form below thunderclouds. Even on their own, thunderstorms can be very destructive. A flash of **lightning** contains a huge charge of electricity with a temperature that can be hotter than the surface of the Sun!

HOW DOES A THUNDERSTORM FORM?

Thunderstorms form where warm, moist air is rising rapidly, usually in summer. The air contains large amounts of **water vapour**. As it rises, the water vapour cools and **condenses** to form a black cloud of water droplets. The air in the cloud is still warmer than the air around it, however, so it continues to rise, carrying the water droplets with it. Some of the moisture in the air freezes to form ice crystals. Strong winds push the water droplets and ice around the cloud.

▼ These hailstones are as large as eggs. They fell on Kansas, USA.

HAIL

Thunderstorms often bring hail. As ice crystals move around inside the thundercloud, layers of ice freeze around them, forming hailstones. They fall to the ground when they become too heavy to stay in the cloud.

▼ A flash of lightning rips through the sky. It only lasts for a few seconds and is followed by **thunder**.

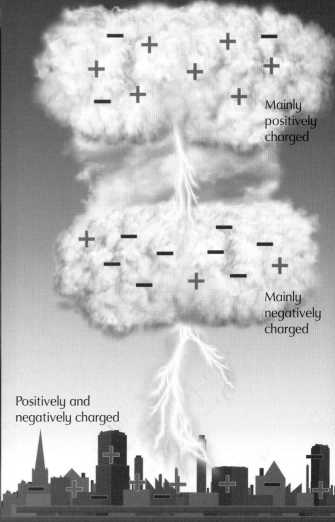

▼ Most lightning leaps from one part of a cloud to another, but some jumps from the cloud to the ground.

Mainly positively charged

Mainly negatively charged

Positively and negatively charged

LIGHTNING AND THUNDER

As the droplets of water and ice crystals are pushed violently around in the cloud, they collide. They rub against each other and become electrically charged. The top of the cloud becomes positively charged and the bottom becomes negatively charged. This creates a giant spark, called lightning. Lightning lasts for less than a second, but it is so hot it makes the air around it suddenly expand. Thunder is the sound of the air being blasted apart.

How does a tornado form?

A tornado is a whirling funnel of air. It usually forms below a thundercloud, but it can also form after a hurricane strikes land. Tornadoes are the most violent type of weather, but usually they only last a few minutes.

▼ A tornado has just begun to form below this heavy black thundercloud.

FIRST SIGNS
The first sign of a tornado could be a green-coloured sky, or light rain that becomes heavy and mixed with hail. A tornado can also form on a clear day with no thunderstorm or hail. The first sign may be dust swirling above the ground.

BIRTH AND DEATH OF A TORNADO

A thundercloud contains strong **updraughts** and **downdraughts**. The strongest tornadoes begin in **supercell thunderclouds**, which have an extremely strong updraught of up to 260 kilometres an hour. Before a thundercloud produces a tornado, the rising air begins to spin. It spins because wind near the top of the cloud is blowing at a different speed or in a different direction from the wind lower down in the cloud. The tornado first appears as a funnel below the cloud. It grows longer and reaches down towards the ground. As the tornado moves across the land, it loses energy. The funnel becomes thinner, the winds slow down and the tornado shrinks back into the thundercloud.

▲ A tornado ends when the funnel shrinks back into the cloud. Clear sky follows behind the thunderstorm.

A CHAIN OF TORNADOES

Tornadoes often occur one after the other. A supercell thundercloud can produce six or more violent tornadoes. In April 1974, the United States experienced the worst outbreak of tornadoes ever. In just 16 hours, 148 tornadoes touched down over 13 states, from Alabama to West Virginia. These deadly twisters killed 330 people and caused major destruction across 4000 kilometres of land.

◀ A tornado at its height. It makes a deafening roar as it travels across the land.

Preparing for a tornado

When thunderclouds form, meteorologists try to assess whether the storm will produce a tornado. They track the storm and use radar to find out whether any of the clouds contain rotating, rising air. When they think a tornado could form, they issue a tornado warning.

UNPREDICTABLE

It is difficult for meteorologists to predict which thunderstorms will produce tornadoes. Even when a funnel has been spotted, it is difficult to work out the path of a tornado because it can change direction at any time.

▼ These meteorologists in Wichita, Kansas, USA, are tracking thunderstorms and tornadoes in Tornado Alley.

▲ The safest place to be during a tornado is in an underground shelter.

TORNADO WARNING

When meteorologists think that tornadoes could form, they issue a tornado watch or a tornado warning. People listen for warnings on radio and television. Some people have weather radios that only come on when there is a tornado warning. When a tornado watch is issued, people bring in any loose objects from outside. When a tornado warning is issued, they find shelter. Many buildings have storm shelters, usually below ground level. If they do not have a storm shelter, people go into an inside room or hallway away from windows and outside doors. Motorists are told to leave their cars and shelter in a ditch. They should not try to escape by driving faster than the storm.

STORM CHASERS

Instead of trying to avoid a tornado, **storm chasers** try to find them. Some storm chasers are tourists, but most are scientists who want to study tornadoes in detail. Storm chasers follow thunderstorms in special vehicles. The vehicles have radar, cameras and other equipment to measure and record the tornado. Storm chasers may follow storms for weeks before they find a tornado. When they do, they try to get as close as possible without getting caught. This is a very dangerous job.

▼ Storm chasers use trucks packed with equipment, including radar, a computer and radio.

Destructive power of a tornado

Tornadoes are also called twisters because the wind spirals in such a tight circle. Most tornadoes are less than 500 metres wide, although the strongest tornadoes may be nearly four times this width. A tornado's path of destruction is much narrower than other storms, but a tornado's strong winds can cause greater damage.

MEASURING TORNADOES

It is not possible to measure the wind speed of a tornado because it is over so quickly. Instead the **Fujita scale** rates a tornado and its wind speed from the damage it causes. The power of the wind increases faster than the speed. For example, a wind of 320 kilometres an hour is four times, not twice, as powerful as a wind of 160 kilometres an hour.

▼ The tornado that struck Greensburg in Kansas, USA, on 4 May 2007 destroyed most of the town and was the worst tornado to hit the country for ten years.

PATH OF DESTRUCTION

Damage from a tornado is limited. The houses on one side of a street may be flattened, while houses on the other side are hardly affected. Cars and mobile homes are easily overturned. The rising column of air in the centre of the tornado sucks up dust and litter, as well as heavier things, such as cars and even people – dropping them many metres away. The strongest tornadoes can last for up to an hour and travel at up to 100 kilometres an hour.

◀ A tornado has sucked this huge tree out of the ground and smashed it into the house.

▶ This house in London, England, was ripped apart by a tornado in December 2006. The houses across the street were undamaged.

FUJITA SCALE

CATEGORY	ESTIMATED WIND SPEED	DAMAGE
0 Light	105 to 137 kilometres an hour	Branches of trees broken
1 Moderate	138 to 177 kilometres an hour	Roofs damaged, broken windows
2 Considerable	178 to 217 kilometres an hour	Large trees blown over, roofs blown off, mobile homes destroyed
3 Severe	218 to 266 kilometres an hour	House walls collapse, cars overturned
4 Devastating	267 to 322 kilometres an hour	Houses totally destroyed, cars lifted
5 Incredible	322 kilometres an hour +	Large buildings damaged, cars thrown more than 90 metres

Strange happenings

A **waterspout** is a tall column of rising air and water. It is a kind of tornado that forms over warm water in the sea or a lake, and moves across the surface. It can cause unusual events, including showers of fish or frogs.

▲ A waterspout in the Gulf of Mexico. Waterspouts usually last between ten and 30 minutes. Most waterspouts are less powerful than tornadoes.

WATERSPOUTS

A waterspout forms when warm, moist air rises quickly above an area of water. It starts as a whirling pattern on the surface of the water and becomes visible when the water vapour in the air condenses to form a column of water drops. As the waterspout becomes stronger, it sucks up water from the surface of the sea or lake. The winds that spin around a waterspout are much slower than around a tornado, probably because the weight of the water slows them down. A waterspout can overturn boats and, when it moves over land, it can become a weak tornado.

DUST DEVILS

A dust devil can arise quite suddenly, usually in a **desert**. There may not even be a thunderstorm or rain. A dust devil begins when the air just above the ground overheats. It rises and begins to swirl. The rising air sucks up dust and sand, which makes it easy to see as it travels across the land.

▲ This dust devil was photographed swirling across land in Potosi District, Bolivia.

RAINING FISH

A waterspout's rising column of air can suck up fish, frogs and other things along with the water. The fish are lifted high into the air and blown along by the strong wind. They may travel for many kilometres before they eventually fall to the ground. On 18 August 2004, the village of Knighton, Wales, was hit by a shower of fish.

◄ Showers of fish and frogs have been reported in many countries around the world.

The aftermath

Hurricanes and tornadoes can leave behind devastated villages, towns and cities. People may be killed and many more injured or reported missing. It can take years to clear up and repair the damage.

▼ Cyclone Larry struck North Queensland in Australia in March 2006. No one was killed, but it caused millions of dollars worth of damage.

DEADLIEST HURRICANES
In 1970, the Bhola Cyclone hit the River Ganges in Eastern Pakistan (modern-day Bangladesh), killing 500,000 people – the highest number of deaths for a cyclone. The deadliest Atlantic hurricane struck the Caribbean in 1780, killing 22,000 people.

▼ Houses in New Orleans that were damaged by Hurricane Katrina are now being repaired. It will take many years before all the work is complete.

WIND DAMAGE

Strong winds lift off tiles or tear off whole roofs and blow down walls. Buildings may be so badly damaged that they are unsafe and have to be rebuilt. A tornado can flatten buildings completely. Strong winds also blow down trees and **power lines**, cutting the supply of electricity. Trees may block roads and railways. Cars and mobile homes can be overturned and smashed. Buildings that are strongly built are most likely to survive a hurricane or tornado.

▲ These temporary homes have been set up by people in Honduras who were made homeless by Hurricane Mitch.

FLOOD DAMAGE

Flood water is usually polluted with dirt and **sewage**, which makes cleaning up more difficult when the water eventually drains away. The storm surge of a hurricane brings the worst flooding. In Bangladesh in November 2007, flooding washed away thousands of villages. More than three million people were affected and millions of pounds were needed to feed and shelter people who had lost their homes.

Are hurricanes and tornadoes increasing?

In the last 20 years, severe hurricanes, floods and droughts have been occurring more often. The most likely reason for this is that the average temperature of the air is increasing. This is called **global warming**.

WHAT CAUSES GLOBAL WARMING?

Global warming is caused by an increase of certain gases, including **carbon dioxide** and methane, in the air. They are called **greenhouse gases** because they trap the Sun's heat, like a giant greenhouse.

People are increasing the amount of greenhouse gases in the air by burning oil, coal and natural gas. Most cars, trucks and aeroplanes burn oil in their engines, and most power stations burn coal, oil or natural gas to produce electricity.

Sun's rays are reflected

Heat escapes

Sun's rays

Sun's rays are trapped, which warms the atmosphere

▲ The Sun warms the Earth and certain gases, such as carbon dioxide, trap some of the heat in the atmosphere. They act like the glass in a greenhouse.

WHAT WILL HAPPEN?

Scientists believe that, unless global warming is controlled, hurricanes, floods and droughts will become even more common. The oceans warm up very slowly, but even a small rise in the temperature of the sea makes it more likely that hurricanes will form and become more severe. Governments and people need to act fast. They need to find new ways of doing things that produce less greenhouse gases. Scientists are developing engines that burn hydrogen instead of oil. Power stations already exist that use the power of the Sun, flowing water and even the wind to produce electricity. None of these produce carbon dioxide.

▲ This is what cars might look like in the future. The cleanest cars will run on hydrogen.

▼ Wind turbines produce electricity without producing greenhouse gases. They work best in windy places, such as out at sea, on open plains or on the top of hills.

WIND TURBINES

The wind can be used to help to reduce global warming by producing electricity without polluting the atmosphere. As the wind turbine's long blades turn in the wind, they make electricity. The largest wind turbines are built in the sea off the coast.

Glossary

BEAUFORT SCALE
Scale that measures the strength, or force, of a wind by its speed. The scale describes the effects of winds of different speeds and goes from force 0, which is no wind, to force 12, which is a hurricane.

CARBON DIOXIDE
One of the gases in the air. Carbon dioxide is also produced when fuel is burned.

CONDENSE
To change from a gas into a liquid.

CROPS
Plants grown by farmers to be used in some way, for example, as food.

CYCLONE
Any violent storm. Storms that are called hurricanes in other parts of the world are called cyclones in Australia, southern Asia and south-east Africa.

DEBRIS
Rubbish, fragments and other things scattered by the wind, an explosion or other event.

DESERT
A region with little rain and few plants.

DOWNDRAUGHT
Wind that blows downwards towards the surface of the Earth.

DUST DEVIL
A small tornado that sucks up dust as it moves across the land.

EQUATOR
Imaginary line around the middle of the Earth, halfway between the North and South poles.

EVACUATE
To leave a dangerous building or area to go to a safer place.

EYE (OF A HURRICANE)
Area of calm at the centre of a hurricane.

EYEWALL
Clouds that surround the eye of a hurricane. The winds are strongest and the rain heaviest in the eyewall.

FLOOD
Water covering land that is usually dry.

FLOOD DEFENCES
Walls and other barriers built to stop water flooding.

FUJITA SCALE
Scale that measures the strength of a tornado from the amount of damage it does.

FUNNEL
Narrow tube; the funnel of a tornado is a narrow column of rising air surrounded by cloud.

GLOBAL WARMING
Increase in the average temperature of the air around the Earth. Global warming is caused by an increase in gases, such as carbon dioxide, in the air.

GREENHOUSE GASES
Gases in the air that trap the Sun's heat. Greenhouse gases include water vapour, carbon dioxide and methane.

LEVEE
Bank built to stop a river overflowing.

LIGHTNING
Flash of light in the sky caused by a huge spark of electricity.

POWER LINE
A heavy wire for carrying electricity.

PREVAILING WINDS
Winds from a particular direction that normally blow over an area.

RADAR
An electronic system that uses radio waves to pinpoint where an object is.

SAFFIR-SIMPSON SCALE
Scale for measuring the strength of a hurricane by the speed of its winds.

SEWAGE
Waste material and water from toilets and drains.

STORM CHASER
Person who seeks out and follows storms, particularly tornadoes and hurricanes, to examine them close up.

STORM SURGE
A rapid rise of sea level caused by storm winds pushing sea water towards the coast.

SUPERCELL THUNDERCLOUD
A thundercloud with a very strong updraught.

THUNDER
Loud noise made by a flash of lightning. The flash of lightning heats the air around it, making it suddenly expand.

THUNDERCLOUD
Tall, dark cloud that can produce lightning and thunder.

TROPICAL
Taking place in the tropics, the part of the world on each side of the Equator between the Tropic of Cancer and the Tropic of Capricorn.

TYPHOON
Tropical storm that begins in the north-west Pacific Ocean and moves west, hitting countries from the Philippines to Japan.

UPDRAUGHT
Wind that blows upwards.

VALLEY
Low land with mountains or hills on each side.

WATERSPOUT
A tornado that moves across the sea or a lake, sucking up water.

WATER VAPOUR
Water in the form of a gas.

WEATHER SATELLITE
Spacecraft that orbits the Earth, photographing clouds and measuring aspects of the weather.

Index